AF693258

Credit Union Loan Professional Handbook

Written by Mary Anne Sauber

Edited and Produced
by Pamela A. Lee

Human Resource
Development Department
CUNA & Affiliates
Madison, Wisconsin

Product #766

KENDALL/HUNT PUBLISHING COMPANY
2460 Kerper Boulevard P.O. Box 539 Dubuque, Iowa 52004-0539

This publication is designed to provide accurate and authoritative information in regard to the subject matter covered. It is sold with the understanding that the publisher, Credit Union National Association, Inc., is not engaged in rendering legal, accounting, or other professional service. If legal advice or other expert assistance is required, the services of a competent professional person should be sought.

Copyright © 1991, by Credit Union National Association, Inc.

ISBN 0–8403–6637–X

All rights reserved. No part of this publication may be reproduced, stored in a retrieval system, or transmitted, in any form or by any means, electronic, mechanical, photocopying, recording, or otherwise, without the prior written permission of the copyright owner.

Printed in the United States of America
10 9 8 7 6 5 4 3

Contents

Preface

If you're new to the credit union loan department, consider this handbook your guide to success. In it, you'll find the basics you need to get started and excel in your position. And if you plan to continue your training, this book will serve as the introduction to more advanced study.

In this handbook you'll find a brief overview of general concepts and skills, an explanation of your most important duties and responsibilities, and a description of what your manager expects. Each chapter also contains self assessments to help you review key ideas, pinpoint your strengths and weaknesses, and initiate discussions with your supervisor. These self assessments give you the opportunity to find out how concepts presented in this handbook are practiced at your credit union. And checklists included throughout the book provide quick and easy references.

Chapter One introduces the credit union movement and provides a general overview. Chapter Two describes the loan professional's role in relation to members and other employees. Chapter Three outlines basic loan professional qualifications, and introduces some of the federal laws that regulate lending. Chapter Four lists loan professional duties and responsibilities. Chapter Five describes communication techniques and other methods that build good relationships with members and coworkers. And Chapter Six presents loan policies and procedures that direct lending practices.

This handbook is designed to assist you, but its true value depends on you. As you read it, mark important sections and write questions in the margins. Use the information presented here as a catalyst for further training. Set goals for improving your work, based on the results of the self assessments you complete. Keep the book handy as a reference. Above all, put to work on the job the information that you learn here.

Acknowledgments

The author expresses special thanks to the following people for their comments and review of this handbook: Lois Hedlund and Dene Gray, Arizona Federal Credit Union; Nancy Warren, Daviess County Teachers Federal Credit Union; Lois Kitsch, Kennedy Space Center Federal Credit Union; Linda Kirschner, Kentucky Credit Union League; Tom McWilliams, Mississippi Credit Union System; Leah Blazer, Western Kentucky University Credit Union; and Legal Department, Credit Union National Association, Inc.

Chapter 1

Who We Are and How We Differ

When people say, "This is *my* credit union," they mean it. Unlike other financial institutions, a credit union is owned and operated by the people it serves. And that is just one of the many features that make your credit union different from any other financial institution.

All credit unions were originally formed by a group of people who decided they wanted to control their own financial destiny. This handful of people—members, not customers—provided the initial capital to start the credit union, pool their money as savings, and make low-cost loans to each other.

Every credit union in the world—including yours—started this way, and the principle of mutual self-help still applies, no matter how large or how small your credit union is now.

How We Differ

Three major characteristics distinguish your credit union from other financial institutions:

1. Your credit union is owned by its members, who democratically control it.
2. Your credit union is a not-for-profit cooperative.
3. Your credit union relies heavily on volunteers for direction.

The aspects of member-ownership and democratic control of your credit union are most important. They are apparent when members use mail ballots to elect directors. And they are apparent at your annual meeting where members meet to hear reports of board and committee members and vote on credit union issues. Each member has one vote—no matter how much or how little money is deposited or borrowed.

Your members also play a key role in setting policy. They elect directors who appoint other volunteers and hire managers to handle day-to-day operations. Figure 1.1 shows a typical credit union organizational chart.

Because it is a member-owned cooperative, your credit union has no inner group of stockholders who benefit personally from its success. After normal operating expenses and allocation to reserves, your credit union's net earnings are distributed to your members as dividends, reduced interest charges,

Figure 1.1 Typical Credit Union Organizational Structure

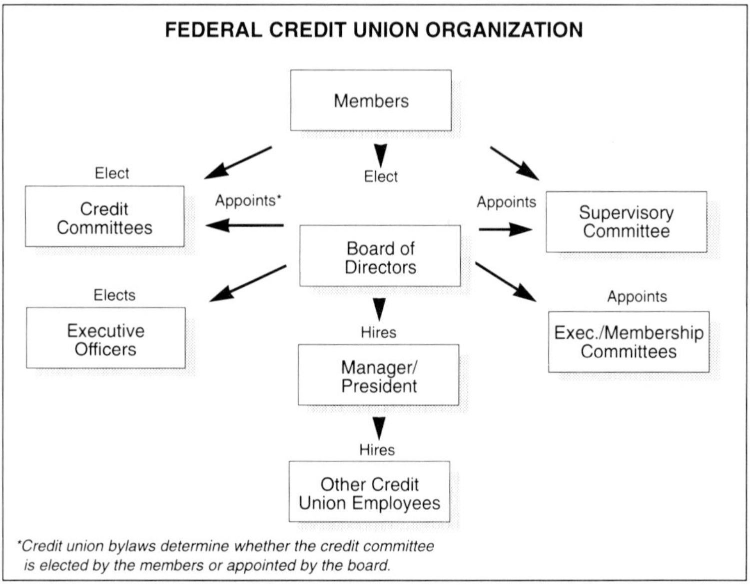

and/or improved services. This is why credit unions and other cooperatives are described as "not-for-profit." They are *not*, however, the same as charitable or "nonprofit" organizations.

Your board of directors and committee members volunteer their time to fulfill the expectations of your membership, ensure quality service, and maintain fiscal safety and soundness. These volunteers are unique in the financial world in that they assume tremendous responsibilities and demanding workloads—in most cases *without* monetary compensation.

Credit Union Facts

To the typical consumer, all financial institutions may look alike. But the fundamental differences discussed above—and those shown in Figure 1.2—help make credit unions an appealing alternative to their "for profit" counterparts. In addition, these credit union facts are important:

- Credit unions provide financial services to many persons who could not otherwise obtain or afford them.
- To help their members make wiser financial services decisions, credit unions educate them about issues affecting their financial well-being.
- The United States credit union movement, through the World Council of Credit Unions, is helping people build a better life in 72 developing countries in the Caribbean, Central America, South America, Asia, Africa, and the Pacific.
- Most credit unions offer loan protection insurance and life savings insurance at no direct charge to their members.
- A credit union's board of directors is made up of volunteers who are elected by the membership and can be replaced when decisions do not reflect the will of the membership.

Figure 1.2 How Credit Unions Compare

THE CREDIT UNION AS A FINANCIAL INSTITUTION

	Credit Unions	Banks	Savings and Loan Assn's	Small Loan Companies	Retail Store Charge Accounts
Orientation or Purpose	Not-for-profit cooperative	Profit	Profit	Profit	Profit
Type of Organization	Democratically controlled cooperative	State or federally chartered corporation	State or federally chartered corporation	Corporation	Local or national corporation
Source of Income	Loans to members and investments	Loans to customers and investments	Loans to customers and investments	Loans to customers	Loans to customers
Distribution of Income	Dividends to members	Dividends to stockholders	Dividends to stockholders	Dividends to corporation investors	Dividends to store's stockholders
Services Offered	Savings and lending plans, share drafts, etc.	Business and personal loans, checking accounts, credit cards, IRA's, etc.	Home mortgages, savings accounts, NOW accounts, etc.	Primarily consumer loans	Primarily consumer loans to purchase items in the store

- Money is safe in credit unions. All deposits up to $100,000 are insured. Historically, the credit union movement has been financially sound, and the credit union system is stronger now than ever.
- Many corporations consider the availability of credit union services an attractive employee benefit, and they often sponsor and support them by providing space and incentives to help start one.
- The credit union movement fosters the establishment of student credit unions to encourage

thrift and consumer education among young people.

- Credit unions are unique not so much in *what* they do, but in *how* and *why* they do it. As member-owned, financial cooperatives, they are unique in the business sector.

Types of Services

Credit unions range in size from less than one million dollars in assets and a few hundred members to billion-dollar institutions providing thousands of members with all types of services shown in Figure 1.3. Which services and how many depend on the size of the credit union and the needs of its members. Generally speaking, credit unions offer the same consumer services as banks and other financial institutions, but terminology may differ. Credit unions, for example, offer "share" accounts, which are similar to savings accounts in other financial institutions. Credit union shares, however, represent the amount of money a person deposits to become a member in a credit union. This amount represents the share of the credit union owned by that member, and the members' shares pay dividends.

Similarly, credit unions offer "share draft" or "share checking" accounts, which are comparable to checking accounts and often promoted as such. The term "share draft" refers to members drafting from share accounts by using a piece of paper—the share *draft*.

It is imperative that you know *all* the services available to your members and that you help find out what other services they may need.

Keeping up with changes in the financial field and knowing what other credit unions are doing is very important—as is relaying comments by your members on what should be offered as new services or as improvements to existing services.

Guiding Principles

Credit union roots go back to the mid-19th century in Germany where Herman Schulze-Delitzsch, a repre-

Figure 1.3 Typical Credit Union Services

TYPICAL CREDIT UNION SERVICES

- Share accounts
- Share drafts
- Money market accounts
- Variable-rate loans
- Payroll deduction
- Automatic teller machines
- Debit cards
- Money orders
- Credit cards
- Drive-through tellers
- Personal loans
- Auto loans
- Wire transfers
- Individual retirement accounts
- Home equity loans
- Night depositories
- Savings accounts
- Installment loans
- Certificates of deposit
- Lines of credit
- Direct deposit
- Deferred compensation
- Share insurance
- Travelers checks
- Pay-by-phone service
- Safe deposit boxes
- Mortgages
- Home improvement loans
- Christmas clubs
- Overdraft protection loans
- Telephone transfers, inquiries
- Business loans

sentative to parliament, worked with city people and Friedrich Wilhelm Raiffeisen, a town manager, helped develop the idea of self-help financial services.

Credit unions were started in North America in the early 1900s by a Canadian, Alphonse Desjardins of Levis, Quebec. Desjardins was a legislative reporter who learned of the dreadful effects usury was having on the people of his country and wanted to help. The credit union, his "caisse populaire" (people's bank), proved to be an ideal way for people to get the loans they needed at affordable interest rates.

The idea soon spread across the border where, with Desjardins' help, the parishioners of St. Mary's Church in Manchester, New Hampshire organized the first credit union in the United States in 1909. With the help of Boston merchant and philanthropist Edward A. Filene and Massachusetts attorney Roy F. Bergengren, the idea spread across the country.

A traditional credit union motto is "not for profit, not for charity, but for service." This motto evolved over the years as people banded together to obtain the financial services they needed, but were unable to get, from established banking systems.

Their guiding principles included *open membership* (any person of good will who falls within the field of membership may join), *democratic control* (all members have an equal say in the operation of the credit union—one member, one vote—regardless of the number of shares owned), *not-for-profit orientation* (after normal operating expenses are paid and funds are set aside for reserves, any net income that remains is returned to the member), and *neutrality* in race, religion, and politics.

The principles that guided these pioneers and still guide your credit union are now known as the *International Credit Union Operating Principles.* They were formally adopted by the World Council of Credit Unions and its national confederations in 1984.

A National Network

Every credit union is linked to the *credit union system,* a national network that will help train and educate your staff and volunteers, offer advice and counsel, support your financial services, and work for your interests in state and federal legislatures. Your most direct link in the system is your state credit union league.

Your state league is a non-profit trade association organized to (a) help you and your credit union with problems; (b) meet your educational and informational needs; (c) work for your legislative interests; and (d) provide a link for your credit union with the rest of the credit union system. Some of the other key components of the system, as shown in Figure 1.4, include the following:

Credit Union National Association, Inc. (CUNA). A nonprofit trade association that provides those programs and services for leagues and credit unions that are best developed on a national basis. These include educational and training materials, workshops, and schools; magazines and newsletters; research; public relations; legislative support; and new product development.

CUNA Service Group, Inc. (CSG). Jointly owned by CUNA and its member leagues, services include credit and debit card programs; share draft, travelers check, and money order programs; individual retirement account programs; national radio, television, and print advertising; and office supplies, forms, custom printing, and specialty items.

CUNA Mortgage Corporation. Provides affordable home financing for credit union members.

U.S. Central Credit Union. A credit union *for* credit unions, it enables credit unions to take advantage of the economies of scale it can provide to manage credit union funds, rather than investing in or borrowing from non-credit-union institutions. It provides access to efficient financial and payment services on local, regional, and national levels.

CUNA Mutual Insurance Group. A group of eight companies that offer different types of insurance to credit union members throughout the world.

World Council of Credit Unions. The international organization of credit unions and financial cooperatives. Supports the growth of credit unions and cooperative ideals in nearly 80 countries through various technical and development services.

Figure 1.4 Credit Union System

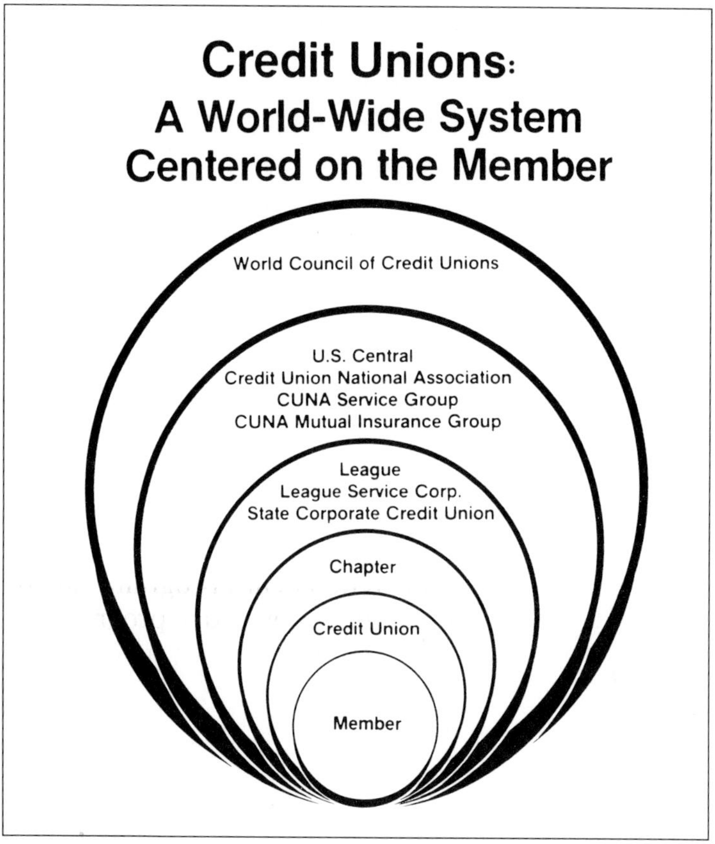

Government Regulation

Credit unions can be chartered by either the state or federal government. All volunteers *must* know all laws—both state and federal—that affect the operations of their credit union, especially because many of these laws deal directly with consumer credit issues.

If your credit union is *state-chartered*, you need to know that most states have state credit union laws that specifically deal with credit union organization and operations. A state agency examines your credit union annually to make sure it is complying with all appropriate laws and regulations, and to make sure it is being operated in a sound and prudent manner. In addition, your credit union will have to operate under a variety of other federal and state laws. If your state chartered credit union is *federally insured,* it may be subject to certain NCUA regulations as well.

If yours is a *federally chartered* credit union (all federal credit unions have the word "federal" in their names), it is supervised and regulated by the National Credit Union Administration (NCUA). The NCUA has exclusive authority governing certain areas of operation of federally chartered credit unions, particularly in the area of loans and lines of credit. Therefore some state laws covering the same subjects will not apply to federally chartered credit unions. You need to know which of your state laws are *preempted* and which ones continue to apply to your credit union.

Headquartered in Washington, D.C., NCUA has six regional offices located throughout the country. Because NCUA examines every federal credit union every year, it also has hundreds of examiners throughout the country.

All federally chartered credit unions are required to provide insurance on deposits up to $100,000. All federal and many state-chartered credit unions are insured by the National Credit Union Share Insurance Fund (NCUSIF). Other state-chartered credit unions are insured by various state and regional cooperative share insurers, and most of these insurers provide the same levels of coverage as the NCUSIF.

These powerful governmental agencies do *not* conduct audits. They examine credit unions for safety and soundness.

The first step in learning more about your credit union is knowing how and why it differs from other financial institutions—knowing that (1) your credit union is owned by its members; (2) your credit union's operation is not-for-profit; and (3) your volunteers play an important role in directing your credit union.

Your credit union is different. Different from any other financial institution. Different from any other credit union. It has a unique history and philosophy—and it is depending on you to carry on the tradition.

Chapter 2

Your Role as a Loan Professional

Your Role Regarding Members

Members depend on credit unions to serve their loan needs. In turn, credit unions depend on loan income to succeed. As a loan professional, you exert tremendous influence over both.

You are the link between members and the money they wish to borrow. Whether members need the money to improve their lifestyles or handle emergencies, obtaining it depends on you. You determine whether or not members will be granted loans—even if you do not make the final decision. Consequently, you play a key role in the credit union's relationship with its members—and ultimately, in the credit union's success.

As a loan professional, you are more than just an application taker. Your role to members is that of financier, counselor and service provider.

As financier, you determine how loans can be best structured to meet members' needs. As counselor, you hear about members' personal debts and any problems associated with them. You also explain when debt can create too heavy a burden and suggest ways to handle it. As service provider, you not only process members' requests, but you also point out additional loan services that may help them as well. Overall, your job is much more than simply completing forms and handing out checks.

Your Role in Other Departments

As a loan professional, you accomplish a variety of tasks when working with members, but your job does not end there. You also have a responsibility to every other department in the credit union because it takes the cooperation of all employees for the credit union to succeed. You and each of your fellow employees share a common goal—to serve members.

To succeed as a team, employees need to know the ground rules, and understand the jobs each coworker performs. That includes you as a loan professional. Each application you process is governed by your credit union's policies and procedures. And with each loan request, you interact with one or more other credit union departments. It is essential, then, for you to know your credit union's policies and procedures, and to be aware of how departments work.

Understanding how other departments function will make you more successful as an employee. When you know how procedures impact the rest of the credit union, you will be more likely to adhere to them. In addition, your understanding will help you answer members' questions about their loan accounts.

Members often expect loan professionals to be money experts. If they have a question about any credit union service, they assume a loan employee can answer it. If possible, you should do so. Members like to have one person handle all their needs. It personalizes their service and saves them time. But if you can't answer a question, admit it and get help. Even with a solid understanding of each department, you will occasionally be asked a question you can't answer. Or, your area may not be set up to accommodate the member's request. If that's the case, it's much better to get help than to waste the member's time.

Depending on their size, most credit unions have the following departments in addition to the loan department: teller counter, member services, accounting, share draft, payroll deduction, investments, collections, personnel and marketing. A brief explanation of each follows.

The *teller counter* handles members' daily transactions. Tellers make deposits, withdrawals and transfers to accounts, according to members' requests. They also accept loan payments, provide balance information, cash share drafts or checks, and sell money orders, U.S. savings bonds, and traveler's checks.

In some credit unions, the more time consuming counter services are performed by a *member services* department. Member service employees open and close accounts. Often, they sell money orders, bonds, and traveler's checks. The member service department sometimes is combined with other departments such as share drafts, investments, and even loans so members can handle most of their business at once. Tellers and member service personnel are the only employees who see members more than loan professionals.

Every loan transaction you complete must be doublechecked and reported by the *accounting department*. With the help of the credit union's data processing system, accounting employees make sure all transactions are classified into categories and posted in the credit union's general ledger. By recording loan transactions accurately at all times, you can help this department.

The *share draft (checking) department* tracks members' share draft accounts by performing such duties as ordering new share drafts, placing stop payments, handling overdrafts and working with monthly statements. When assisting members with their loan needs, you may hear questions about share draft accounts. Try to help first, but if the problem requires research or you are unsure of how to solve it, know who can help and call that person immediately or direct the member to the appropriate location. You will also receive applications for overdraft protection.

Members access this type of loan only when they overdraw their share draft accounts. To process overdraft protection requests, you need to review members' share draft account histories and work with the share draft department in setting up the loans.

The *payroll deduction department*, which may be part of the accounting department, is responsible for tracking and applying the amounts members designate to be deposited automatically into their accounts from their payroll checks. Correctly completed payroll deduction cards are critical. Incorrect cards are a serious source of error in deductions, and when errors are made, members understandably become angry.

Because loan payments are often made through payroll deduction, you will help members complete their cards and possibly even use the computer to set up deductions. Your knowledge of how to divide monthly loan payments, according to how often the members are paid, is vital to correctly completing payroll cards. You should also be able to explain how other deductions are affected by payroll frequency. For example, if a member is paid twice a month, has a $175 monthly loan payment and requests $50 to go into a share account, explain that $87.50 will be deducted for the loan each payday. Then verify that the member wants $50 to go into the share account *each* payday, not once a month.

Investment services at each credit union vary, but usually an *investment department* offers certificates of deposit, individual retirement accounts and money market accounts. All of these accounts earn higher dividends than regular share accounts because they require either minimum balances, minimum time on deposit, or both. As a loan professional, you may require some loans to be share secured. This means the credit union uses certain investments as collateral for these loans.

The *collections department* is directly linked to your work as a loan professional. Collections employees are responsible for contacting members who are slow in repaying their loans. In many cases, members are difficult to locate so collectors depend on the accuracy, detail, and completeness of information you take during the loan application. They also depend on legal access to collateral pledged against loans in event of default. To ensure their access, you must complete the proper documentation when you set up the loan. When making arrangements with members who are slow in repaying loans, collectors may suggest a one-month extension, reduced payments or a consolidation of bills. As a loan professional, you will assist members with their applications for these arrangements.

Another credit union department is *personnel* (or human resources), which handles your employee records, payroll and benefits at the credit union. Your responsibility to this department is to notify it promptly whenever information changes on your personal records, such as your address, home phone or family status, which might affect your medical coverage, your life insurance beneficiary or your pension program. You are also responsible to provide any required documents, such as timesheets, doctor's statement of illness, or vacation requests, promptly and according to policy. Whenever you aren't sure of what is required, it's *your* responsibility to ask questions. Your credit union may also offer a variety of training opportunities through this department.

The *marketing department* develops promotions for the credit union. It encourages members to use additional services by advertising these services through the mail, on the radio or television, in publications or at the credit union itself. It may also educate members with a periodic newsletter. Since many credit union promotions are for loan services, it is important for you to be aware of the promotions and be prepared to explain them to members. You can assist the marketing department by showing members how your credit union's programs and products can help them.

These departments and their activities may vary from one credit union to the next, depending on the credit union's size. If you would like to learn more about any of your credit union's departments, ask your supervisor. Find out if you can observe in other departments before the lobby opens or during slow times of day. Look into training videos or books your credit union may have describing what each department does. Ask if you can read the procedures manual for different departments. If other loan employees are interested as well, check the possibility of having someone from another department attend a meeting of your department to answer your questions. No matter which option you choose, your supervisor will probably appreciate your desire to learn more.

Your Role in Relation to Management

In addition to members and other departments, you must maintain a good working relationship with your credit union's management. From the time you start your job, management has certain expectations of you as an employee. They may be in your job description. However, these expectations aren't always communicated, but they exist nevertheless. To continue working as a loan professional, you need to know these expectations and strive to fulfill them. The six areas of expectation established by management and shown in Figure 2.1 are: *attendance*, *confidentiality*, *loyalty*, *dedication*, *honesty* and *knowledge*.

Proper *attendance* is the most basic expectation management has of its employees. Getting to work on time and being present every day show how seriously you take your job. Being punctual means being at your station—not the coffee pot—when you're scheduled to start work. It also means returning from lunch and breaks on time. It's a good idea to arrive at the credit union several minutes early. That way, you have time to greet coworkers, get coffee and check your grooming. None of these should be done during scheduled working hours. Avoid cutting your travel time to the credit union so close that you arrive at the last minute. Unexpected events such as heavy traffic, a train, bad weather or car trouble may cause you to be late.

Plan to be at work every day you are scheduled. Typically, management staffs the credit union with the minimum number of employees needed to serve members, so when you're absent, service suffers and your fellow employees are overworked.

Naturally, there will be days when you are too ill to work. Management understands. But a sick day should be used only when you are truly ill and not simply because you've accumulated another sick day. When you must be absent, call your supervisor as early as possible before the start of the work day so other arrangements can be made at the credit union. Try to schedule routine doctor and dentist appointments on days you don't work. If that is not possible, ask your supervisor in advance for the day and time that would be least inconvenient. Finally, find out your credit union's attendance policies and follow the guidelines for absences.

Confidentiality is the second expectation. For any financial institution's employees, confidentiality is a critical part of professional behavior. A credit union professional does not discuss credit union business outside work. Members' finances and the policies that pertain to them are confidential. Never compromise your members' trust in you. Confidentiality also means keeping information about your own earnings to yourself and not discussing it with fellow employees.

Management's third expectation is *loyalty*. As long as you work at the credit union you should support its policies. Privately, you may not always agree with them. But publicly, you represent the credit union, and any disagreement you show members is confusing and destructive. As a loyal employee, you must remain supportive at all times.

Members will frequently share their opinions or questions about financial situations with you. While it is not necessary to give management a detailed report of every comment, you should relay important ones. Since you see members every day, management depends on you to relay this information. It helps management make improvements in the credit union and plan for the future.

Dedication is management's fourth expectation. Dedicated employees work beyond their minimum job requirements. When assigned tasks are completed, they ask for more work instead of simply trying to look busy. They are not clock watchers. Dedicated employees volunteer for after-hours work. They become involved with credit union activities, such as their local league or chapter meetings. They attend training sessions or classes during their own time.

The fifth expectation is *honesty*. At credit unions, honesty is particularly important due to the nature of the business. Management relies on you to keep financial accounts completely accurate and to avoid the temptation of taking any cash. You should also avoid taking home any supplies that belong to the credit union—no matter how small they are. If you make a mistake on a loan and can't correct it by yourself, admit it to your supervisor so it can be rectified. Follow policies at all times. Never bend the rules to make a loan. If you are offered any type of compensation to make sure a loan is approved, report it to your supervisor immediately. Above all, tell the truth.

Management's sixth expectation is that you have job-related *knowledge*. Lending is regulated by a number of laws, and management expects you to comply with them. Your credit union has operational policies and procedures. One of your priorities is to learn and follow them. In chapters that follow lending regulations and policies and procedures will be discussed in more detail.

The six areas shown in Figure 2.1 are the primary expectations management has of loan employees. As a loan professional, it is your responsibility to meet these expectations.

Your Role in the Credit Union System

As a credit union loan professional, your role reaches beyond members, coworkers and management. You and your employer are part of the entire credit union system—a network of financial cooperatives and their support organizations all dedicated to serving members' financial needs. You contribute to the overall system, making it stronger or weaker depending on the quality of your work. Other loan professionals do the same.

Assisting you—and credit unions throughout the country—are support organizations such as your state league, your corporate credit union, U.S. Central Credit Union, and the Credit Union National Association, Inc.

Figure 2.1 Management's Expectations

MANAGEMENT'S EXPECTATIONS OF LOAN PROFESSIONALS

Attendance

- Be at your work station on time
- Plan for unexpected delays
- Take sick days only when necessary
- Schedule medical appointments on your own time

Confidentiality

- Never discuss credit union business outside of work
- Never compromise your members' trust in you
- Avoid discussing earnings with coworkers

Loyalty

- Support credit union policies
- Never criticize your credit union in public

Dedication

- Keep busy
- Volunteer for additional duties
- Be active in credit union functions
- Look for training opportunities

Honesty

- Keep accurate records
- Never take cash, supplies or bribes
- Admit mistakes
- Be truthful

Knowledge

- Know lending regulations
- Follow all policies and procedures

SELF ASSESSMENT

Your Knowledge of Members

DIRECTIONS: List four ways in which members expect you to fulfill each of the loan professional roles listed below.

A. You are a financier when you...

1. ____________________
2. ____________________
3. ____________________
4. ____________________

B. You are a counselor when you...

1. ____________________
2. ____________________
3. ____________________
4. ____________________

C. You are a service provider when you...

1. ____________________
2. ____________________
3. ____________________
4. ____________________

Discuss your answers with your supervisor. Write any additional ideas the two of you share.

____________________	____________________
Your Signature	Supervisor's Signature
____________________	____________________
Date	Date

SELF ASSESSMENT

Your Knowledge of Other Departments

DIRECTIONS: For each credit union department listed, rate yourself on how knowledgeable you are about what it does and how it operates.

Department	Ratings				
	Thoroughly Informed				Not at All Informed
1. Teller Counter	5	4	3	2	1
2. Member Services	5	4	3	2	1
3. Accounting	5	4	3	2	1
4. Share Draft	5	4	3	2	1
5. Payroll Deduction	5	4	3	2	1
6. Investments	5	4	3	2	1
7. Credit card	5	4	3	2	1
8. Collections	5	4	3	2	1
9. Personnel	5	4	3	2	1
10. Marketing	5	4	3	2	1

For any department you rated a 3 or less, find out who can help you learn more. Discuss your need with your supervisor, and set a deadline by which you can accomplish your goal.

	Department to Research	Contact Person
1.	______________________	______________________
2.	______________________	______________________
3.	______________________	______________________

______________________ Your Signature

______________________ Supervisor's Signature

______________________ Date

______________________ Date

SELF ASSESSMENT

Your Knowledge of Management

DIRECTIONS: Rate the statements below according to your opinion of management's highest expectations. Use 1 for the expectation you believe is most important, 10 for the least important. Then ask your supervisor to do the same. Discuss your answers together.

Management expects me to . . .	**Your Rating**	**Supervisor's Rating**
1. Always tell the truth.	________	________
2. Comply with all lending regulations.	________	________
3. Be on time to work every day.	________	________
4. Volunteer for additional work.	________	________
5. Support all policies, even if I don't agree with them.	________	________
6. Schedule medical appointments on my own time.	________	________
7. Become involved in credit union activities.	________	________
8. Maintain accurate records.	________	________
9. Maintain confidentiality about members' loan accounts.	________	________
10. Attend extra training sessions.	________	________

____________________	____________________
Your Signature	Supervisor's Signature
____________________	____________________
Date	Date

Chapter 3

Getting and Keeping Your Job

By now, it's clear that a loan professional's job is both challenging and demanding. The person who chooses this position must be well qualified. Successful loan professionals possess these six qualifications: *people skills, organizational skills, persistence, flexibility, professional appearance* and a *positive attitude*.

People Skills

Loan professionals like people. They enjoy working with others. Unlike some employees who prefer to work independently, loan professionals are comfortable working with members—chatting with them, hearing their concerns and exploring ways to help them with their financial needs.

Working with members successfully requires *people skills*: remaining objective, listening carefully, explaining clearly, interviewing thoroughly, showing understanding and remaining patient. Loan officers must also be discreet because members often tell them confidential problems.

Organizational Skills

Loan professionals also need to *be organized*. Every approved loan requires documentation. Even loans that are denied require certain forms. To maintain accurate files, you must keep records organized. Each loan you process will be in a different stage of completion, so keeping files orderly is essential. Staying organized helps members receive their money quickly and efficiently. It also helps ensure that the credit union's loans meet legal requirements.

Organizational skills include *attention to detail.* The old saying about making sure all the "i's" are dotted and the "t's" are crossed holds true in lending. At the very least, oversights can create delays with loans, causing members to become angry. In some cases, missed details may mean the credit union's loss of any claim to its collateral on a delinquent loan.

Persistence and Flexibility

Being persistent is another skill loan professionals need. The information required for loan decisions may not always be easy to find. Staying with the task until it is finished is an important part of your responsibilities. In addition, structuring some loans to meet both the members' needs and the credit union's policies requires not only creativity, but persistence as well.

Flexibility is also a skill you should have. In lending, your job priorities may change according to the number or type of loans waiting to be processed. Likewise, members may change their minds about what they want. Or, a coworker's absence may cause responsibilities to shift. Whatever the reason, you need to be ready for unexpected events.

Part of being flexible is the *ability to remain calm under pressure.* Loan professionals should be able to work well even when members are waiting or become irate. Not every situation will be pleasant or evenly paced. Some days will be slow while others will be extremely busy. It's your job to remain pleasant in these situations.

Professional Appearance

Members base their first impression of you on your appearance. Since first impressions are difficult to counteract, you must take special care to communicate your professionalism with the way you look. Consider that members reveal their personal finances to you and receive your advice about them. Your appearance should inspire their trust. To convey your seriousness, the clothing you wear should be conservative. Generally, suits, blazers with skirts, or sports jackets with pants are most appropriate. Wearing a suit coat or blazer coordinates your look and is most businesslike. However, other appropriate items include: solid dress pants and long-sleeve shirts with conservative ties; dress skirts with matching long-sleeve tailored blouses or sweaters with subtly patterned scarves; long-sleeve pullover sweaters with dress shirts and ties; sweater vests over long-sleeve shirts or blouses; tailored dresses with long sleeves or three-quarter length sleeves. Colors and patterns should be muted and subtle.

As a general rule, dark, solid colors or pinstripes are more conservative. Avoid wearing denim or fleece material, and anything sleeveless or low-cut. If the material on the shirt or blouse you're wearing is thin, be sure to wear an undergarment. Don't assume your jacket will cover any flaws. Keep in mind that trendy clothing is not always professional. Try to stick with more classic styles on the job. Your credit union may have its own dress code; check its requirements and adhere to them.

Professional clothing is an investment. Since you will not be able to use your casual wear at work, you will need to spend some of your salary on business apparel. But because a conservative look will enhance your professional success, a business wardrobe is well worth the investment.

Grooming is also an essential part of your appearance. If your clothing is businesslike but your grooming is poor, you send a conflicting message to members. Keep your hair neat and clean. Men should trim mustaches and beards frequently. Women should apply makeup lightly. Keep your nails well manicured and short, and your hands clean. Be sure your shoes are polished, and avoid wearing too much jewelry. Remember that you need to achieve a conservative look. Heavy makeup or a trendy hairstyle conveys the opposite impression.

Gum and snacks affect your appearance as well.

Make it your rule never to chew gum on the job. Even discreet chewing detracts from a professional appearance. Snacks and beverages should also be kept away from your work area. Smoking, too, is inappropriate. If you smoke, do so only during breaks and lunch.

Your work station is part of your appearance as well. Keep your area neat and organized. Replenish applications, brochures and other forms promptly. Don't display cartoons, jokes or other inappropriate decor. Save personal items for your home.

Positive Attitude

A final qualification for loan professionals is a *positive attitude*. Your actions and appearance are governed by your attitude, so it is vital to keep a positive outlook at all times. When you expect work to be enjoyable, it usually is. Also, problems can more readily be solved when they are approached positively. However, when you look for difficulties, you'll find them. Remember, your job does not just happen to you. You make it what it is.

Your attitude also influences the people around you. Coworkers will respond more pleasantly when you are cheerful. Even under stress, other employees will remain calm more often when you keep your cool. When you refrain from making dissatisfied comments about work, your coworkers will not complain as frequently either.

Members, too, are affected by your attitude. Most will respond in the same manner as they are treated. If you remain positive, even angry members will usually calm down.

Maintaining a positive attitude also means staying objective. Lending decisions must be based on facts, so it is important that you avoid jumping to conclusions about members and their lifestyles. Not every member will share your values or beliefs. Strive to keep an open mind and to avoid being influenced by factors that have no impact on loan decisions.

A sense of humor is another key ingredient of a positive attitude. Seeing the humor in difficult situations—without treating them lightly—helps you remain positive. It also helps you control stress.

Personal concerns strongly influence your attitude at work. Naturally, if you start the day arguing with someone at home or fighting traffic on the way to work, you will find it more difficult to stay positive on the job. However, worrying about home problems during work will only detract from your performance at work. Concentrate on leaving personal concerns outside as you enter the credit union. Then, use your time commuting home to focus your thoughts back on personal concerns. If you are experiencing a serious personal problem, you may wish to inform your supervisor.

Keeping a positive attitude will make your job more enjoyable. Adding the other qualifications, as shown in Figure 3.1, will help you be successful as a loan professional.

Figure 3.1 Loan Professional Qualifications

LOAN PROFESSIONAL QUALIFICATIONS

People Skills

- Work well with people
- Help others
- Be discreet

Organizational Skills

- Maintain accurate files
- Pay attention to detail

Persistence

- Stay with tasks until completed
- Structure loans to meet needs

Flexibility

- Be ready for unexpected events
- Stay calm under pressure

Professional Appearance

- Wear conservative and business-like clothing
- Practice good grooming
- Avoid gum and snacks

Positive Attitude

- Expect work to be enjoyable
- Treat others cheerfully
- Leave personal concerns at home

Legal Considerations

As a loan professional, your work is regulated by a number of federal and state laws. Keeping your job depends on your compliance with them at all times. Loan decisions, documentation and repayment are all affected by these laws. Consequently, your members and your employer trust you to know and obey all legal requirements. If you do not comply, either knowingly or unknowingly, you may cause your credit union to be liable for fines and other legal penalties. Your job depends on being thoroughly familiar with all lending regulations. You will need additional training from your credit union or league, but here is an overview of the most comprehensive federal laws that apply.

Equal Credit Opportunity Act

The Equal Credit Opportunity Act (ECOA) is part of a broad federal law designed to protect consumers' credit rights, called the Consumer Credit Protection Act (CCPA). ECOA was established to prohibit discrimination in credit transactions. It lists nine areas in which discrimination is illegal. They are: sex, marital status, race, color, religion, national origin, age, receipt of protective income, and exercising in good faith any right under CCPA. ECOA affects all aspects of the lending process—from the application, to the loan interview, to the evaluation of the member's creditworthiness. To help loan professionals comply with ECOA, the Federal Reserve issued Regulation B. This regulation specifies what creditors must do to avoid discrimination. Regulation B also requires creditors to notify applicants of loan decisions, and to provide the reasons for loan denials.

Truth-in-Lending

Another part of the Consumer Credit Protection Act is a law called Truth-in-Lending. This law was designed to help consumers understand credit terms and compare credit offers from different lenders. It is implemented by Regulation Z.

Regulation Z provides details on how to disclose the cost and terms of consumer loans. To comply, your credit union uses special loan documents designed to meet these disclosure requirements. The regulation also governs credit advertising, credit card issuance and unauthorized usage liability, borrowers' rights to cancel credit arrangements, and the Fair Credit Billing Act.

Fair Credit Billing Act

To protect consumers from unfair billing practices, the Fair Credit Billing Act was created. It details the procedure creditors must follow when an amount to be paid is in dispute. It also allows consumers to delay paying the disputed amount until the procedure is completed.

Fair Credit Reporting Act

The Fair Credit Reporting Act was established to protect consumers' rights regarding their credit histories. Credit reporting agencies collect data about how consumers repay their loans and credit cards. The data is compiled into reports and made available to creditors for a fee. Because these credit reports are a key factor in loan decisions, inaccurate information could prevent consumers from receiving additional credit. Therefore, the Fair Credit Reporting Act requires agencies to allow consumers to review their files, investigate possible errors, correct existing errors and include consumer statements on disputed reports. The law also requires lenders to inform consumers when credit requests are denied because of information on credit reports.

Fair Credit Practices Act

The Fair Credit Practices Act became effective in 1987. This law specifies several security provisions that federal credit unions are prohibited from including in their loan contracts. It also prohibits assessing additional charges on late fees which have not been paid when due. In addition, this law requires that a notice be given informing potential cosigners of the obligation they will be undertaking.

Other Lending Laws

A number of other federal laws also regulate lending. Among them are:

- Uniform Commercial Code
- Uniform Consumer Credit Code
- Federal Fair Housing Law
- Real Estate Settlement Procedures Act
- Home Mortgage Disclosure Act
- National Flood Insurance Act of 1968

Some of these laws concern home mortgage lending, which is not discussed in this handbook. For more information about all federal and state laws that affect your work, consult your credit union or league.

ECOA, Truth-in-Lending, and other legal requirements discussed in this chapter are all federal laws. Much of your job will be affected by them, as well as by a number of state laws. To comply with all lending regulations, you must know them. For more information, check with your supervisor.

Self-Improvement

With any job, continually looking for ways to improve is the mark of a true professional. You can demonstrate your professionalism by accepting additional job duties, completing seminars or classes, and participating in credit union functions. Handling more responsibilities shows your desire to grow in your job. Attending additional training and functions such as your credit union's annual meeting or your league's chapter meetings indicates your commitment. The Credit Union National Association, Inc. and your state league provide many training opportunities. Taking the initiative to improve your job skills will greatly enhance your continued career success.

SELF ASSESSMENT

Qualifying as a Loan Professional

DIRECTIONS: Circle the number which indicates how frequently each statement below describes you.

	Always				Never
1. I remain objective about members, regardless of their lifestyles or appearances.	5	4	3	2	1
2. I maintain accurate files at all times.	5	4	3	2	1
3. The clothing I wear to work is businesslike.	5	4	3	2	1
4. I enjoy listening to members and exploring ways to help them with their loan needs.	5	4	3	2	1
5. I never smoke, eat or drink at my work station.	5	4	3	2	1
6. When job priorities change unexpectedly, I respond quickly and efficiently.	5	4	3	2	1
7. I comply with all lending regulations.	5	4	3	2	1
8. On any day at work, I treat coworkers and members cheerfully.	5	4	3	2	1
9. I am able to find the humor in situations, even those that are difficult.	5	4	3	2	1
10. I persist with tasks until they are completed.	5	4	3	2	1
TOTAL POINTS	______				

Scoring:

45 - 50 points — Excellent work! Keep it up!

36 - 44 points — You are doing well in most areas. Concentrate on increasing the low items.

25 - 35 points — Improvement is needed. Identify why certain areas are difficult and begin working at them.

24 points or below — Examine your desire to work as a loan professional. You probably would be better suited to another job.

SELF ASSESSMENT

Lending Laws

DIRECTIONS: Ask your supervisor for additional information about each of the laws listed below. Then list four specific actions that must be taken on the job to comply with each law.

A. Equal Credit Opportunity Act
1. ______________________________
2. ______________________________
3. ______________________________
4. ______________________________

B. Truth-in-Lending
1. ______________________________
2. ______________________________
3. ______________________________
4. ______________________________

C. Fair Credit Billing Act
1. ______________________________
2. ______________________________
3. ______________________________
4. ______________________________

D. Fair Credit Reporting Act
1. ______________________________
2. ______________________________
3. ______________________________
4. ______________________________

Discuss your answers with your supervisor. Write any additional ideas the two of you share.

______________________	______________________
Your Signature	Supervisor's Signature
______________________	______________________
Date	Date

Chapter 4

Your Duties and Responsibilities

Loan professionals are not limited to a few routine tasks. Their duties and responsibilities are numerous, often changing pattern each day to meet members' needs. Common loan professional duties are listed below. Depending on your credit union, you may perform some or all of these duties.

Loan Professional Duties

- Take loan applications
- Verify application information
- Run credit bureau reports
- Calculate loan payments
- Determine collateral values
- Obtain loan payoff information
- Answer loan questions
- Analyze application and credit information
- Make loan decisions
- Perfect liens on collateral
- Inform members of loan decisions
- Prepare loan documents
- Disburse loan checks
- Obtain members' signatures on loan documents

At your credit union, the list of duties may be somewhat different. Use the Self Assessment at the end of this chapter to record your duties and to determine how well you perform each of them.

Loan Professional Responsibilities

Your responsibilities as a loan professional should be met while you perform each of your duties. As a loan professional you must

- Maintain good relations
- Comply with all legal requirements
- Follow credit union policies and procedures
- Maintain confidentiality
- Find all relevant facts
- Keep accurate documentation
- Stay objective
- Match lending services to members' needs
- Be ethical

Maintaining good relations is your most important responsibility. Good loan service begins with treating members courteously. Take the time to give each member warm, personal attention. All members deserve respect. Even if they become angry, stay calm and show them courtesy.

Legal compliance is another of your important responsibilities. Almost every duty you perform is affected by one or more lending regulations. Disobeying these laws can result in serious fines and other penalties for your credit union, so you must not take them lightly. Learn how each law specifically impacts your job and comply with its requirements at all times. See Chapter Three for more information.

Following credit union policies and procedures is vital, too. They are designed to protect the membership from loan losses, ensure consistency and comply with the law. As a loan professional, you are expected to know these rules and adhere to them. If you disagree with a policy or procedure, don't disregard it. Discuss it with your supervisor. If you are tempted to make an exception for a long-time member or personal acquaintance, think again. To ensure fairness, all members must be treated consistently. While you may help one person by ignoring a rule, you may be hurting the rest of the membership.

Your fourth responsibility is to *maintain confidentiality*. Members trust you with detailed information about their personal finances and credit history. The status of members' loans, the amounts they request, and their credit histories are all confidential information. Members expect you to keep this information private. *Never* discuss one member's finances with another. Among coworkers, limit such conversations only to employees who need to know. At those times, be aware of your surroundings. Members' information should be discussed only in a private area—not where it can be overheard by other employees or members. Never discuss credit union business in a social setting.

Fact finding is another responsibility you have. Loan decisions are based on facts. Missing or incorrect information can lead to improper decisions. As you perform your loan duties, take the time to gather and accurately record all relevant facts. When members are unable to provide immediate answers, mark the application for follow up. When verifying information, be prepared to contact several sources if necessary.

The next responsibility you have is to *keep accurate documentation*. Relying on your memory for details about members' loans is too risky. Not only are you likely to forget the information, but other employees may need it when you're not available to ask. In addition, written proof is required whenever the credit union's claim to repayment or collateral is questioned. To keep your loan files accurate, ask your supervisor for a list of documents that should be included.

Your seventh loan professional responsibility is to *stay objective*. It's human nature to make quick judgments about people based on their appearances or actions. It's also easy to be influenced by a member's troubles. However, basing your job performance on attitudes or beliefs instead of facts compromises the credit union's position. To treat all members fairly, you must remain objective and control your personal feelings.

Matching lending services to members' needs is the next responsibility you have. When members request a loan, your job is not only to process their application, but to determine if another loan or credit union service could benefit them as well. Often, members are unaware of these services. By pointing out services, you expand members' options and show them other ways their needs can be met. A member who regularly applies for loan amounts under $500, for example, may benefit from a credit card or a revolving line of credit. Another member who lists a car loan with a different financial institution on their loan application may appreciate your suggestion to refinance the vehicle for a lower rate at the credit union.

The final loan professional responsibility is *being ethical*. Business ethics are based on the values of honesty and loyalty. Ethical employees do not take advantage of their positions for personal gain. Your good judgment should tell you whether or not you are taking advantage of your position. For example, accepting a bag of homemade holiday cookies from a member would be perfectly all right. So would keeping a complimentary ballpoint pen from an insurance representative. However, accepting any gift for more than small, token value, particularly if it is exchanged for the way you have handled a loan, is unethical and illegal. Your credit union will have additional rules that deal with this area of employee conduct.

Good judgment should also tell you that making a short, toll-free personal call during your break is fine, but placing toll calls at the credit union's expense is not. Stocking your desk at home with paper clips and pens from the credit union may seem harmless, but it goes beyond the boundaries of honesty and integrity.

Practicing good business ethics also means being careful not to discuss credit union business outside work. Credit union security practices are confidential information. Telling your friends that one member owes over $20,000 in credit cards, for example, or that another member has previously filed for bankruptcy, is intolerable.

Being ethical is an important part of your job, as are the other responsibilities of a loan professional. Performing your responsibilities and duties, as shown in Figure 4.1, is a continual challenge, but makes your job rewarding as well.

Figure 4.1 Duties and Responsibilities

DUTIES AND RESPONSIBILITIES OF LOAN PROFESSIONALS

Duties

- Take loan applications
- Verify application information
- Run credit bureau reports
- Calculate loan payments
- Determine collateral values
- Obtain loan payoff information
- Answer loan questions
- Analyze application and credit information
- Make loan decisions
- Perfect liens on collateral
- Inform members of loan decisions
- Prepare loan documents
- Disburse loan checks
- Obtain members' signatures on loan docments

Responsibilities

- Maintain good relations
- Comply with all legal requirements
- Follow credit union policies and procedures
- Maintain confidentiality
- Find all relevant facts
- Keep accurate documentation
- Stay objective
- Match lending services to members' needs
- Be ethical

SELF ASSESSMENT

Handling Your Loan Professional Duties

DIRECTIONS: In the left-hand column, check each duty that you perform as a loan professional at your credit union. Write in any additional duties. Then, decide how much you know about the duties and check the appropriate boxes.

Duty	**I can perform this duty:**		
	Very well	With help	Not at all
☐ Take loan applications	☐	☐	☐
☐ Verify application information	☐	☐	☐
☐ Run credit bureau reports	☐	☐	☐
☐ Calculate loan payments	☐	☐	☐
☐ Determine collateral values	☐	☐	☐
☐ Obtain loan payoff information	☐	☐	☐
☐ Answer loan questions	☐	☐	☐
☐ Analyze application and credit information	☐	☐	☐
☐ Make loan decisions	☐	☐	☐
☐ Perfect liens on collateral	☐	☐	☐
☐ Inform members of loan decisions	☐	☐	☐
☐ Prepare loan documents	☐	☐	☐
☐ Disburse loan checks	☐	☐	☐
☐ Obtain members' signatures on loan documents	☐	☐	☐

Other Duties

☐ ______________________________	☐	☐	☐
☐ ______________________________	☐	☐	☐
☐ ______________________________	☐	☐	☐
☐ ______________________________	☐	☐	☐

Use this checklist to help you improve your work. For any duty you do not know how to perform well, write down what you can do to increase your knowledge. Then set a goal for yourself, writing the date by which you will be able to perform the duty successfully. Discuss results with your supervisor.

Goal	**Deadline**
1. ____________________	________________
2. ____________________	________________
3. ____________________	________________
4. ____________________	________________

____________________ ____________________

Your Signature Supervisor's Signature

____________________ ____________________

Date Date

SELF ASSESSMENT

Handling Your Loan Professional Responsibilities

DIRECTIONS: Use this self assessment to determine your strengths and weaknesses in handling your loan professional responsibilities. Circle the number that best describes what you do, from 5 (meaning *always*) to 1 (meaning *never*).

	Always				Never
1. I am courteous to each member who talks to me.	5	4	3	2	1
2. I am familiar with all laws that affect my work and I comply with them.	5	4	3	2	1
3. I follow credit union policies and procedures.	5	4	3	2	1
4. I discuss members' information in private areas, and only with the members themselves or coworkers who need to be informed.	5	4	3	2	1
5. I submit loan requests only after I have found all the necessary facts.	5	4	3	2	1
6. I maintain all my loan files with proper documentation.	5	4	3	2	1
7. I do not allow personal attitudes about members to interfere with my judgment.	5	4	3	2	1
8. I look for ways to help members with other credit union services, and suggest them whenever possible.	5	4	3	2	1
9. I refrain from discussing credit union business outside work.	5	4	3	2	1
10. I limit personal calls to toll-free numbers, and make them only when necessary.	5	4	3	2	1
TOTAL POINTS	______				

Scoring:

45 - 50 points	—	Super! You are a thoroughly responsible loan professional!
36 - 44 points	—	You are successfully performing most of your responsibilities. Work on areas that received a 3 or less.
25 - 35 points	—	Immediate improvement is needed. Reread this chapter and set specific goals for changing your job performance.
24 points or below	—	You are not handling your job responsibilities adequately. It's time to seriously consider another occupation.

Chapter 5

Your Relationships and Communication

Excellent loan service depends on the relationships you form with others. How you act on the job is determined largely by how you *interact* with members, coworkers, supervisors and managers. Therefore, building good relationships is beneficial both to you and the groups of people you work with daily. When you relate well with them, you'll find more enjoyment in your job, which in turn means you'll provide better service.

Feeling positive about the members you help makes your work more rewarding. The atmosphere becomes more relaxed when you and your coworkers assist each other. Likewise, productive relationships with your supervisor and manager increase your self-confidence and encourage you to set higher standards.

The key to building and maintaining good relationships is communication. Since effective communication is a two-way process, it involves listening as well as talking. Unfortunately, many people don't realize this. To them, communication only means getting their ideas across. True communication, however, is an exchange of ideas. In the loan department, this exchange occurs when members convey their needs and loan professionals explain their services. Only with this type of exchange will communication occur.

Communication Techniques

Effective communication in the loan department includes these nine techniques:

1. Make and maintain eye contact
2. Smile
3. Greet the members
4. Use names
5. Listen actively
6. Rephrase for understanding
7. Ask questions
8. Take notes
9. Close pleasantly

Eye contact is the most fundamental way to let members know you are listening. By looking them straight in the eyes as they talk, you let them know that what they say is important to you. Likewise, when you maintain eye contact with members as you talk, you inspire their trust in what you say.

Smiling is the best way to communicate positively without saying a word. Smiling is universally understood as an expression of interest and friendliness. With each person, your smile will set the tone for a positive encounter.

Greeting the person breaks the ice and begins the formal relationship between you. Let others know you are happy to meet them by standing up, shaking hands firmly and welcoming them to the credit union. Then take a few moments to chat. This helps put people at ease and creates a more comfortable atmosphere.

Using people's names is an effective way to personalize your message. It demonstrates that they are important to you as individuals. People who hear their names are also more likely to listen to your message since you are directing it specifically to them.

Listening actively is vital to any successful communication. When you listen actively, you focus your attention completely on what the speaker says. You let the speaker know you are concentrating by using either nonverbal gestures such as nodding your head, or short remarks such as "Oh," or "I see." Active listening helps you avoid the temptation to interrupt or allow your thoughts to wander, so you can truly hear the speaker's message.

The technique that complements active listening is *rephrasing*. Once you have heard the message, rephrasing it in your own words lets both you and the speaker make sure you understand. Rephrasing inspires others' confidence in you because it demonstrates your desire to be accurate with their information.

Asking questions is another important communication technique for loan professionals. Open-ended questions elicit the most information because they cannot be answered with a simple "yes" or "no." Open-ended questions begin with these words: *who, what, when, where, why*, and *how*.

Taking notes also strengthens communication. Loan professionals process a tremendous amount of information. Trying to recall all the details of an interview or conversation may be difficult. Notes help you retain important facts. Remember, however, that notes written on the application become part of the member's loan file, which is subject to examination. Keep your notes in compliance with all regulations.

The final communication technique is *closing pleasantly*. Since people remember the beginning and end of an interaction most clearly, it is important to finish positively. Summarize what has occurred. Allow the other person to add any final thoughts. Let that person know you appreciate the time spent communicating with you, and if needed, schedule a follow-up appointment. No matter how busy you are, take enough time to conclude the interaction pleasantly.

These nine communication techniques, as shown in Figure 5.1, form the basis of good relationships with members and employees. However, other techniques are important as well.

Figure 5.1 Communication Techniques

NINE TECHNIQUES FOR EFFECTIVE COMMUNICATION IN LENDING

1. Make eye contact
2. Smile
3. Greet the person
4. Use the person's name
5. Listen actively
6. Rephrase for understanding
7. Ask questions
8. Take notes
9. Close pleasantly

Relating to Your Members

With members, five techniques will further strengthen your relationships. The techniques are shown in Figure 5.2:

- Be courteous
- Use tact
- Maintain confidentiality
- Avoid jargon
- Explain terms

Courtesy is a basic part of providing good service. Members deserve to be treated with respect. After all, they own the credit union. Without them you would not have your present job. When you're under pressure, that may be easy to forget. Instead of giving members your attention, you may be tempted to treat them as an interruption. If that happens, think about how you expect to be treated in department stores or restaurants. Recall situations when clerks ignored you or acted rudely. More than likely, you became angry. You may even have decided not to return.

Members share the same attitudes about service. They expect you to show good manners, no matter how rushed you are. Whether or not they return with more business depends on how courteously you treat them.

Tact is also part of maintaining good relationships with members. Being tactful is simply taking the time to polish what you say. Consider members' feelings as you choose your words. For example, if you must ask about repayment problems that a member has listed, you will not create a favorable reaction by saying, "Why were you so late paying your bills last year?" Instead, you could say, "I noticed some repayment difficulty last year. What seemed to cause the trouble?" By using tact, you can get your message across and keep the atmosphere positive as well.

Maintaining confidentiality is another important part of relating to members. As mentioned earlier, always discuss members' business with them in a private area. Even then, speak in a reserved tone of voice. Keep your desk clear of other members' files when you are working with someone else. And never mention one member's business to another.

Avoiding jargon is also a good idea when working with members. Jargon—financial terminology that is part of your job—makes sense to you because you use it daily. To members, though, it does not. Telling them you will "cut a check" or that they are "upside down on their car loan" is confusing. And when you use jargon, you put members in an awkward situation. They must either admit their ignorance and ask you to explain what you said, or they can pretend to understand and leave with unanswered questions. Neither choice strengthens your relationship with them. Although members may not notice when you *avoid* using jargon, they will find your statements easier to understand. That in itself will promote better relations.

The final technique is to *explain terms*. Sometimes in lending, jargon is unavoidable. This is particularly true during loan closing, when you are directed by law to disclose the requirements of the loan before the borrowers sign any documents. In these situations, take care to spend enough time discussing each term. Watch members for any nonverbal actions that may signal confusion, such as frowning, fidgeting, or staring off in one direction. Use simple, clear language without "talking down" to them. And be aware of your voice. Once explanations become repetitious, it's easy to switch to a monotonous tone which is both impersonal and hard to follow. Concentrate on varying your explanations, and put expression in your voice.

Figure 5.2 Member Relations

RELATING TO MEMBERS

1. Be courteous
2. Use tact
3. Maintain confidentiality
4. Avoid jargon
5. Explain terms

Special Situations with Members

Not every encounter with members is routine. As a loan professional, you will often face unique situations. These situations may challenge your ability to provide good service. How you handle them will determine your continued relationships with the members involved. Figure 5.3 summarizes the suggestions to follow.

Telephone

Loan professionals often work with members over the telephone. Members call for a variety of reasons. They ask about loan rates and vehicle values, inquire as to decisions about their applications, even apply for loans at some credit unions. Talking to members over the telephone requires special techniques.

The first technique is to *concentrate on personal service*. Being physically separated from members creates an impersonal climate. As a result, you must work harder to provide personal service. Add more expression to your voice. Speak pleasantly and use the member's name often. And smile frequently. Even though members can't see you, they can hear the smile in your voice.

Then, *remain focused*. Since the member is not in front of you, it's easy to become distracted by your surroundings. It's also easy to let your mind wander. Either way, you can miss valuable information. To prevent distraction, select a focal point and concentrate on it as the member speaks.

Next, *clarify and verify information*. Over the telephone it's more difficult to hear. Speak clearly and at a slower rate than you do in person. Rephrase information to check for understanding. And if you pause to calculate a payment or find a vehicle's value, explain what you're doing. Each of these steps shows members that you care enough to make sure they understand.

Finally, *use telephone hold manners*. Members usually call to save time. When you cause them to wait by placing them on hold, they can become impatient. Consequently, you should avoid using the hold button whenever possible. If you must, ask before placing them on hold. Explain why you must leave the phone and wait for their response. Then return within one to two minutes and thank them for waiting. An alternative to placing members on hold is to obtain a phone number and call them back.

Irate Members

One of the least pleasant aspects of your job is dealing with irate members. Members become angry for any number of reasons. They may have waited too long to see a loan employee. A loan officer may have denied their credit request. The members may disagree with a policy or an error may have occurred when setting up the loan.

Whatever the cause, such members demonstrate their displeasure in no uncertain terms, and that behavior naturally causes anxiety among loan professionals. Your first response may be to take their anger personally. Don't. Even if you are responsible for the problem, allowing members' anger to affect you will only complicate matters. Try instead to view such members as a challenge, not a threat. Then, use these techniques.

First, *stay calm*. Ignore the "fight or flight" instinct. Don't refuse to listen to the member, and don't argue. Don't ignore the member's complaint or avoid eye contact. Concentrate on remaining calm and assisting the member with the problem.

Second, *listen*. Members who are upset want to get the problem off their chests. Focus on what they say and do not interrupt. If you jump in quickly, they can become angrier.

Third, *show understanding*. Let them know you can identify with their situation. Say, "I can understand why you feel frustrated." This personalizes the confrontation and demonstrates your willingness to help.

Fourth, *identify the problem.* Make sure you know exactly what has happened to cause the anger. Rephrase what you have heard to clarify it.

Fifth, *solve the problem.* If you can't solve it, get your supervisor or someone who can. And take time to explain the situation to the other employee so the member doesn't have to repeat it all again. Be prepared to get help, too, if you see that the member will only be satisfied by speaking to someone with more authority, or if a member becomes abusive.

If the member is not satisfied with your solution, tactfully ask, "What would you like to have done?" Then you can hear what the member expects and determine if that solution is possible. Such an option may not have occurred to you. Sometimes, though, your credit union's policies may prevent you from offering the solution the member wants. Tactfully explain the policy to the member and, if possible, offer other options.

Sixth, *keep your mood positive.* Challenge yourself to prevent the member's anger from affecting you. Don't let one episode spoil your service to other members.

Waiting Members

Another stressful part of your job occurs when members are waiting for loan service. Even if your credit union's procedure is to schedule loan appointments, unexpected events can create backlogs. One member may arrive late, another early. Some members have more questions and take longer than the time you estimated they would need. And sometimes mistakes occur within the credit union in preparing paper loan documents, causing you to be unprepared when members arrive on time.

In any case, members who wait become understandably annoyed. Knowing that, a loan professional's first response is to speed up so that members can get through more quickly. While that intention is good, such a response will only compound the problem, since being hurried through after being made to wait will anger members more. Also, pressuring yourself to work faster may cause you to leave out steps you would normally take. As a result, more mistakes can occur. The best solution is to keep a steady pace and use the following techniques:

First, *stay calm; don't get anxious.* Remind yourself that you can only help one member at a time, and each member deserves your complete, courteous and accurate service.

Next, *acknowledge the waiting members.* As you call one member from the waiting area, smile at the others and tell them they will be helped soon. This lets them know you have not forgotten them.

Remember to *stay pleasant.* You may be busy, but now more than ever it's important to greet each member cheerfully. Apologize to them for the wait, and thank them for their patience.

Get back-up help. If help is available, the best time to call for it is when you begin to get behind. Find out your credit union's procedure ahead of time.

Overall, *stay positive.* Sometimes, no matter what you do, members who have been waiting get upset. As you continue working with them, they still may not have calmed down. When you finish with them, apologize again for the wait, thank them, and meet the next member with a pleasant attitude.

Denials

For many loan professionals, the most difficult part of their job is informing members when credit has been denied. Telling members "no" is uncomfortable. And if you personally disagree with the decision or sympathize with the member's situation, denying them is particularly unpleasant.

Keep in mind, however, that a denial may be in the member's best interest. A new debt may overburden the member. The techniques that follow will also help.

First, *inform members of the decision*. Don't prolong the uncertainty. Members want to know the outcome as soon as possible.

Second, *explain the reasons*. Tell members why their loan was denied. They deserve to know and it is their legal right. To explain more clearly, be sure you understand the reasons before talking to members.

Third, *pause*. Give members a moment to let the news sink in. Resist the temptation to relieve your discomfort by filling the silence with words. Members need time to respond. Expect a variety of reactions —disappointment, anger, confusion. By pausing, you give members the opportunity to share their feelings with you.

Fourth, *answer questions and suggest alternatives*. Once you have broken the news, don't cut members off. They may need to hear you repeat the reasons for denial. Or, they may have questions you can answer. Furthermore, they may appreciate any other options you can suggest.

Fifth, *remain positive*. Even if members become irate, stay calm and pleasant. Consider how you would feel in their situation. Talk to members in a pleasant tone of voice, but at the same time, be firm. Don't promise that a future application will be approved if circumstances change. And if members become abusive, get your supervisor.

Children

Children often accompany their parents to loan meetings. And with their short attention spans, they quickly lose interest and become bored. As a result, even the best-mannered children can misbehave, first distracting their parents and, finally, disrupting the entire meeting.

Your job is to help children behave and keep their parents happy. Your credit union may have a children's table where kids can play while they wait. If not, ask about keeping a supply of inexpensive "busy toys" on hand. Then give the child a toy when the meeting begins. Or, if you distribute candy or balloons, remember to do so at the beginning instead of at the end, but be sure to get permission from the parent first. In a pinch, you can give the kids notepaper and a pencil to draw, or let them play with a calculator. Finally, if nothing works and the parents are unable to concentrate, suggest scheduling another appointment at a later time. Remember, successfully handling children will strengthen your relationship with parents.

Elderly

Another special group of members is the elderly. Remember that increased age does not mean decreased intelligence. Older people may have physical limitations, but they should not be treated as if their mental capabilities are limited. Do not patronize the elderly. Treat elderly members with the same respect you show others. If they have difficulty hearing or take more time, be patient. Do all you can to help them.

Handicapped

As with the elderly, members who have physical handicaps are no less intelligent than others. Never talk down to handicapped members or avoid communicating with them. If you think they need special assistance, be sure to offer it, but avoid being overly helpful. Ask members if they would like your help, rather than giving it without asking. Handicapped people value their independence and do not appreciate others who automatically do for them what they have worked hard to do for themselves. Remaining sensitive to their needs and treating them with respect are two of the greatest services you can give.

For additional training in handling these and other special situations, check with your supervisor.

Figure 5.3 Special Situations

HOW TO HANDLE SPECIAL SITUATIONS

Telephone
- Concentrate on personalizing your service
- Remain focused
- Clarify and verify information
- Use hold manners

Irate Members
- Stay calm
- Listen
- Show understanding
- Identify the problem
- Solve the problem
- Keep your mood positive

Waiting Members
- Stay calm, don't get anxious
- Acknowledge waiting members
- Stay pleasant
- Thank members for their patience in waiting
- Get back-up help, if possible
- Stay positive

Denials
- Inform members of the decision
- Explain the reasons
- Pause
- Answer questions and suggest alternatives
- Remain positive

Children
- Look for ways to occupy the children
- Reinforce positive actions

Elderly
- Do not patronize
- Treat with respect
- Be patient

Handicapped
- Never talk down or avoid communicating
- Offer assistance, but avoid being overly helpful
- Be sensitive to special needs
- Treat with respect

SELF ASSESSMENT

Member Relations

DIRECTIONS: Each situation below is one that can occur as you work with members. Think about how you would handle each case, then write your response on a separate sheet of paper. Discuss questions or problems with your supervisor.

1. During a loan interview, you ask a member the purpose of a loan he is requesting. He tells you it is personal. You tactfully ask him to be more specific. He becomes angry, saying he has been a member at the credit union for twenty years, has always repaid his loans on time, and it's none of your business. What do you do?
2. You have members scheduled to see you every twenty minutes for the next three hours. The member with you now has already taken thirty-five minutes and isn't finished yet. From your desk, you can see one member waiting. Another is walking in. What do you do?
3. The members before you have brought their toddler and infant son with them to the loan closing. From past experience, you know this meeting will take at least fifteen minutes. The toddler is whining and the baby is fussy. What do you do?
4. You are speaking to a member over the telephone and you need to look up her current loan balance. You ask to put her on hold. She tells you no, she is in a hurry, and the last time she called the credit union she was put on hold for ten minutes. What do you do?
5. You walk into the lobby and call the next member's name on your list. He stands, and you notice the seeing-eye dog beside him. What do you do?

Relating to Your Coworkers

Although your members are your first priority, your coworkers are important too. You and your fellow employees comprise a team, working together to give your members excellent service. To be successful, you depend on other staff as much as on your own abilities. In turn, they depend on you. Therefore, it is in everyone's best interests to establish good relationships with other employees.

Unprofessional behavior in front of your members causes a loss of credibility and respect that may not be immediately apparent, but will seriously damage your credit union just the same. It is considered unprofessional to criticize your coworkers, to gossip and to spread rumors. Respect the contributions your coworkers make and treat them fairly.

Socializing with coworkers is a normal part of your job. Chatting briefly as you start the day or exchanging pleasantries on a coffee break helps foster good relationships and improves your rapport. Be careful, however, not to turn brief chats into ten-minute conversations. It's easy to lose track of time, especially when the coworker is someone you like. Wasting time socializing is unprofessional and causes resentment among fellow employees who are using the same time to work.

Gossip is damaging in any degree. At the very least, it is unprofessional. In some cases, it can ruin careers. Make it your rule not to participate in gossip.

New Employees

New employees feel the same way you did when you started work. There is so much to learn that the new employee can become overwhelmed. You can help by showing support. Welcome your new coworker with a cheerful greeting each day. Make it a point to learn and use the person's name. Include the employee in the lunchtime conversation. Be prepared to explain procedures several times. Remember, what is easy for you now seemed difficult in the beginning.

Difficult Employee Behavior

You may encounter employees who do not take professional behavior as seriously as you do. You may find yourself working with someone who displays a negative attitude about everything, gossips chronically, or does not do a fair share of work. If so, stay positive and focus your attention on remaining professional. Avoid adding fuel to their fires with your own complaints or rumors. And when possible, keep your distance.

With employees who do not contribute fairly, ask yourself how their behavior affects you. If their inactivity bothers you, but your workload remains the same, concentrate on doing your job well and don't worry about theirs. However, if their behavior creates a greater workload for you or endangers members' accounts, consider discussing the problem privately with your supervisor.

In these cases, your intention is not to be a tattletale, but to relay facts that have a great impact on your job or on the credit union. Whatever you do, don't keep these concerns bottled up inside you. Ask your supervisor or another manager for help.

Relating to Your Supervisor

Pleasing the supervisor is usually first on an employee's list of objectives. After all, your supervisor is the one who evaluates your performance, and determines whether to promote, retain or dismiss you.

Trying to meet your supervisor's expectations demonstrates your desire to achieve, your willingness to follow directions and your awareness that success is a team effort. But sometimes it is difficult to know how to build a good relationship. Here are four techniques, as shown in Figure 5.4, that you can use to strengthen your relationship with your supervisor: show respect, follow rules precisely, handle criticism well, and register complaints properly.

First *show respect.* The credit union is not the military, but your supervisor does have authority;

therefore, you should show a proper amount of respect. Avoid talking negatively about your supervisor with coworkers. Such comments always seem to find their way back to the person being discussed.

Second, *follow rules*. Showing your supervisor that you can be counted on to comply with procedures will go a long way in establishing your reliability.

Third, *handle criticism well*. The day will come when your supervisor reprimands your performance. How you handle criticism tells your supervisor a lot about your character. Stay calm. Listen without interrupting. If you need information clarified, ask matter-of-factly; do not become defensive. Decide whether or not you think the supervisor is right. If you did make a mistake, admit it, apologize for it, and assure your supervisor you will work hard not to let it happen again. If you disagree, state what happened calmly. If your supervisor can't see it your way, do not argue. When the discussion is over, resolve to make what changes are necessary, then forget it.

Fourth, *register your complaints properly and appropriately*. Think before you complain. Ask yourself if the problem will solve itself, or if it really interferes with your job. In other words, complain only

Figure 5.4 Supervisor Relationship

RELATING TO YOUR SUPERVISOR

1. Show respect
2. Follow rules precisely
3. Handle criticism well
4. Register complaints properly and appropriately

when you must. Otherwise, you will be seen as the problem.

When you do complain, talk to your supervisor privately. State your opinion in a calm, unemotional voice and offer alternatives to the problem. Don't belabor the discussion. Once you are confident your supervisor understands your view, get back to work and put the conversation behind you. Know the chain of command, and never go over your supervisor's head until you've given him or her a chance to resolve the problem.

Relating to Other Departments

At the credit union, your relationship with employees in other departments should, above all, focus on cooperation. All employees have duties and responsibilities. Showing your understanding that their work is important and that their jobs are also important will help foster the spirit of cooperation and team effort.

Whenever possible, remember to include co-workers from other departments in your conversations. At after hours get-togethers, make a point of mixing with everyone, not just other loan professionals. It's normal to feel most comfortable around those with whom you spend the most time, but refusing to include others leads to cliques.

Relating to Management

Become familiar with the organizational chart in your credit union showing the chain of command. Attend your annual meeting. Ask for additional reading material on the duties of credit union management.

Then, when your president or a board member passes you in the aisle or lobby, take the initiative to greet them. Don't be intimidated by titles. Your president, officers, and directors—like everyone else—will appreciate your friendliness and recognition.

SELF ASSESSMENT

Coworker Relations

DIRECTIONS: Read each statement below. Circle the choice which best describes how often each statement applies to you.

1. I limit chats with coworkers to three minutes or less.	Always	Sometimes	Never
2. I remain patient when coworkers make mistakes.	Always	Sometimes	Never
3. When another employee complains about the job, I try not to join in.	Always	Sometimes	Never
4. I can handle criticism from my supervisor without becoming defensive.	Always	Sometimes	Never
5. I follow credit union rules.	Always	Sometimes	Never
6. I greet each employee I see in the morning.	Always	Sometimes	Never
7. At credit union functions, I visit with many different employees.	Always	Sometimes	Never
8. I refrain from spreading rumors about coworkers.	Always	Sometimes	Never
9. Before I make suggestions, I think them through carefully.	Always	Sometimes	Never
10. I work hard to cooperate with other departments.	Always	Sometimes	Never

SCORING: Give yourself 5 points for each item you marked *always*, 3 points for each item you marked *sometimes*, and 1 point for each item you marked *never.*

Scoring:

45 - 50 points	—	Super! You're relating very well to other employees.
36 - 44 points	—	Good work overall. Concentrate on your low areas.
25 - 35 points	—	Improvement is needed. Determine why certain areas give you trouble and work to correct them.
24 points or below	—	You need to reassess why you became a loan professional. If this score truly describes your conduct at work, you probably would be better off somewhere else.

Chapter 6

Loan Policies and Procedures

Policies are established by the credit union's board of directors to guide day-to-day operations and to comply with federal and state regulations. Policies are usually kept in the form of a written policy manual that is updated regularly.

The board sets policies for many areas of the credit union, but lending is frequently one of the most detailed. Loan policies are the guidelines your credit union uses to direct its lending practices. As part of the credit union's overall policies, they are established by the board of directors to accomplish four objectives: comply with federal and state laws, handle loan accounts fairly and consistently, provide efficient service, and limit the credit union's risk. While policies must comply with the law, they may be more restrictive as long as they do not discriminate.

In providing you with sound, written policies, your credit union's management expects you to adhere to them at all times. Consequently, you must be completely familiar with all loan policies. And since the board periodically reviews and updates them, you need to be aware of any changes when they are made. Failure to learn these loan policies puts your credit union and your job at risk.

Procedures are the methods used to implement policies. Procedures are created by credit union management and are developed from proven techniques. Some procedures are written, others are verbally explained.

Following loan procedures promotes consistency and accuracy as members' credit requests are processed. Although they do not require the board of director's approval, loan procedures are part of your job duties and should be followed unless your supervisor makes an exception.

Sample Loan Policies

Your credit union may have a few simple loan policies or a large number, depending on what the board of directors establishes. Typically, though, policies are written for the areas listed below. However, within your own credit union, be sure to check for the specific rules in these areas.

- Loan authority. This specifies who is able to make loan decisions and what limits, if any, they have in granting credit. In some credit unions, a credit committee rules on all loan applications. In others, loan granting authority is delegated to loan officers.
- Loan amounts. The maximum secured and unsecured amounts members may borrow are stated.
- Credit information requirements. Here, an outline is given of the information members must provide before credit can be extended.
- Credit granting guidelines. This explains how credit requests are analyzed.
- Security. Types of acceptable collateral are listed.
- Interest rates and repayment terms. The board sets its own rates and maturities up to the maximum legal limit.
- Maintenance and review of files. Specifications are stated for periodically updating and checking credit information in members' files.

SELF ASSESSMENT

Loan Policies

DIRECTIONS: Answer each statement below by marking *yes* or *no*. For each item marked *yes*, write the loan policy below the statement. For each item marked *no*, find out the policy and write it in.

I know my credit union's loan policy for:

	Yes	**No**
1. Acceptable types of security	☐	☐
2. The maximum limit on unsecured credit	☐	☐
3. This quarter's interest rates and repayment terms for new car loans	☐	☐
4. The information members must provide before credit can be granted	☐	☐
5. Credit file maintenance and review	☐	☐

Your Signature

Supervisor's Signature

Date

Date

Determining Creditworthiness

Although specific loan policies and procedures vary among credit unions, all financial institutions establish guidelines for determining borrowers' *creditworthiness*—the degree to which they deserve credit. The loan professional evaluates creditworthiness after gathering all the necessary information for making a loan decision. During this evaluation, three factors are analyzed most thoroughly. These factors are referred to as the Three C's of Lending: Character, Capacity and Collateral.

Character

For credit unions, *character* is considered the most important of the Three C's. This has been true ever since credit unions were founded over one hundred years ago to provide low cost loans to members. Today, the single greatest indicator of character is the credit bureau report. It is explained later in this chapter. Other indicators of character are:

- length of member's current and previous residence
- length of member's current and previous employment
- proximity of member's personal references
- credit union's past experience with the member

Each of these items reflects character by demonstrating the member's *stability*. Members who remain at the same residence and job for long periods of time show perseverance, much like the kind they'll need to repay a loan. Also, members who stay in the same place aren't as likely to leave town suddenly without repaying their debts.

If members' current residence and employment are short, previous ones become important. These past records reflect whether members have difficulty staying put, or if they simply made a recent change after years at the same location.

The distance between members and their personal references is another indication of stability. When members are able to list nearby relatives and friends, they demonstrate how settled they are in their community.

Stability is also shown in the credit union's past experience with members. Established members hold long-term share or share draft accounts. They may also have had previous loans that they repaid on time.

While each of these factors indicates stability, loan professionals must remember to look for an overall pattern when evaluating character. Extenuating circumstances can weaken one factor without detracting from a strong overall pattern. For example, a job transfer can cause the member's residence to be recently changed. Or, a career move would make the member's current time on the job short. Many members have one weak stability factor. The key is to make an assessment based on the combination of all factors.

Capacity

A member's *capacity* is the ability to repay. Even if character is strong, a member who lacks the means to repay the credit union should not be granted a loan.

To determine the member's capacity, you must first receive an account of monthly income and all monthly debt obligations. Included as obligations are any current loans at financial institutions, all credit cards, medical bills and the monthly housing payment. Typically, the member lists these debts on the credit application.

Using this information, calculate two debt-to-income ratios. For the first ratio, total the monthly debts, including a payment on the requested loan. Don't include the monthly housing payment. Divide this total by the monthly income (take-home pay, bonuses, interest, dividends, rental income). For the second ratio, use the same steps but include the monthly housing payment among the debts.

Example:

Ratio No. 1

Monthly debts	
Auto loan	$215
Credit cards	60
Requested Loan	+ 150
Total	$425
Monthly income	
Take-home pay	$1,600
Interest	+ 50
Total	$1,650

$425 ÷ $1,650 = 26%

Ratio No. 2

Monthly debts	
Auto loan	$215
Credit cards	60
Housing payment	300
Requested loan	+ $150
Total	$725
Monthly income	
Take-home pay	$1,600
Interest	+ 50
Total	$1,650

$725 ÷ $1,650 = 44%

The ratios indicate how much monthly income members spend to pay debts. The higher the percentages, the less members have left for their remaining budgets. Some credit union policies recommend that the first ratio not exceed 25-30%, and the second 40-50%. Others accept higher ratios provided members have adequate savings to meet emergencies. Acceptable ratios also vary depending on whether credit union policy specifies gross or net income. However, if debt ratios exceed established limits, members' capacity to repay is questionable. Find out the standards at your credit union.

Collateral

The last of the Three C's is *collateral.* Credit unions lower their risk on loans by obtaining collateral whenever possible. Collateral acts as security for repayment. In other words, members pledge something of value to the credit union until their loan is repaid. If they default, the credit union can take possession of the collateral, sell it, and apply the proceeds to the loan balance. However, because of the extra work involved with repossessions, as well as the possibility of lower resale value, collateral is more effective when it remains with members, acting as an incentive for repayment.

Some common types of collateral are: cars, trucks, boats, travel trailers, real estate, stocks and shares. Members' loans can also be secured by other people acting as cosigners. They agree to repay the loan if a member defaults. Cosigners and other forms of collateral should never be used to overcome a poor credit risk. Instead, they should be used to make good loans better.

Before accepting collateral, loan professionals should determine its accurate value. Valuation books for many types of vehicles are available to assist you. Depreciation is another factor to consider. If the collateral will depreciate faster than the unpaid loan balance, the term of the loan may be too long.

The credit union's claim to collateral must be legal. Security agreements signed by the members help ensure the credit union's right to repossession. Liens—written claims placed on titles of ownership—also provide legal proof.

Your credit union has policies and procedures for valuing collateral as well as securing it. Become familiar with these rules.

Credit Bureau Reports

The strongest evidence of members' characters can be found in their credit bureau reports. Most creditors provide credit bureaus with the repayment histories of their borrowers. The bureaus act as clearinghouses for credit records, compiling information and providing it to lenders for a fee. Their reports include a listing of creditors, how they have been repaid, outstanding balances, collections and repossessions, employment records, and legal transactions of public record.

Loan professionals usually obtain credit bureau reports by computer. They enter information about the member into the credit union's terminal and it is transmitted to the credit bureau. Minutes later, a report prints out.

Credit bureau reports provide an excellent indication of a member's debt paying habits. They also show how much credit the member is accustomed to carrying. By comparing the report to the member's loan application, you can determine if the member has neglected to list any current balances owed. Finally, you can look for evidence of pyramiding debt, where the member acquires several new debts, all within recent months.

Other Tools

Your credit union may use additional methods for analyzing members' creditworthiness. Among these tools are a credit scoring system and a credit profile. A credit scoring system is unique for each financial institution. It is developed using data from the institution's own loan files. Based on this data, points are assigned to factors associated with both current and delinquent loans. When these factors appear on new requests, the same points are applied. Total scores indicate whether the new loans are likely to be repaid on time or become delinquent.

A credit profile is a quick analysis tool used to help loan professionals determine whether applications need additional research. It is similar to a credit scoring system because it is based on information from the credit union's own loan files. Unlike credit scoring systems, however, credit profiles may not be statistically sound.

SELF ASSESSMENT

Credit Analysis Skills

DIRECTIONS: Decide how much you know about the credit analysis skills below and check the appropriate boxes.

	I can perform this skill:		
	Very Well	With Help	Not at All
1. Calculate debt-to-income ratios	☐	☐	☐
2. Determine new and used vehicle values	☐	☐	☐
3. Calculate loan payments	☐	☐	☐
4. Interpret credit bureau reports	☐	☐	☐
5. Verify employment listed on loan applications	☐	☐	☐
6. Verify references listed on loan applications	☐	☐	☐
7. Verify accounts at other financial institutions listed on loan applications	☐	☐	☐

Now use this checklist to help you improve your work. Meet with your supervisor to discuss any skills you do not know how to perform well. Set a goal for yourself, writing the date by which you will be able to perform the duty successfully. Discuss results with your supervisor.

Goal	**Deadline**
1. ______________________________	______________________
2. ______________________________	______________________
3. ______________________________	______________________
4. ______________________________	______________________

______________________________	______________________________
Your Signature	Supervisor's Signature
______________________________	______________________________
Date	Date

Making Sound Decisions

Not all loan policies are clear cut for every situation you will face. At times, you will need to make decisions based on your credit union's policies but using your own judgment. Here are some tips to help you make sound decisions:

1. Get the facts. Make sure you understand exactly what the member is requesting.
2. Refer to credit union policies and procedures. Look for direction from established guidelines.
3. Check your notes. It's a good idea to keep important notes in easy reach. A situation may have been discussed at a staff meeting or during training. If so, you may have a record of it.
4. Remember past experiences. Think about any previous situations that may have been similar.
5. Look for consistency. Ask yourself if what you plan to do is consistent with other credit union practices.
6. Ask for advice. If you're in doubt, check with your supervisor. Excuse yourself and discuss the situation with your supervisor away from the area where the member is waiting.

Using these steps will help you make sound decisions in the loan department. Fortunately, making decisions becomes easier with experience.

The Credit Committee

Many credit unions have a credit committee that is responsible for ruling on members' loan applications. It is made up of members of the credit union, either elected by their peers at the credit union's annual meeting or appointed by the board of directors.

Credit committee members follow lending regulations and the credit union's loan policies in making their decisions. As a credit union grows, the committee may delegate loan-granting authority to loan officers. Usually a maximum loan limit is established for each loan officer based on the individual's experience and expertise. However, questionable loans are referred to the credit committee for evaluation and the committee makes decisions on any loan denials.

If your credit union has a credit committee, it is important that you develop a good relationship with the committee members. Working together to avoid any misunderstandings can ensure that nothing interferes with your mutual goal of lending money to members.

Following Rules

The importance of following policies and procedures should be clear. As explained in preceding chapters, many times these rules are based on federal and state laws, and disregarding them can jeopardize your credit union by causing it to be out of compliance. As a result, fines or other serious penalties may be imposed.

Rules are also established for the safety of funds. Skirting the rules puts funds at risk and negates the trust members have placed in you.

Finally, following rules ensures consistency. Because of the credit union's unique democratic philosophy, members expect equal treatment. To apply rules to one member and not to another is unfair.

Maintaining Flexibility

Keep in mind that policies and procedures are also established to give the credit union flexibility in handling accounts. In many ways, they are unique to each individual credit union, based on laws and the best interests of its members.

There will occasionally be situations that require exceptions to policies and procedures. The key to successful handling of these situations is to obtain a supervisor's approval. Never override a policy on your own. If you feel an exception is warranted, consult someone in authority.

Explaining Policies to Members

Sometimes members will question why a policy exists. They may be angry about a rule you are enforcing. Or, they may simply want clarification. At any rate, you should be able to explain credit union policies effectively to your members. To do so:

1. Understand the policies. Ask questions if they don't make sense. You won't be able to explain what you don't understand.
2. Keep your explanation brief and clear. Don't cloud the issue with information that doesn't apply.
3. Stress the *benefits* to members. Show how the policy is designed to protect the best interests of all members.
4. Offer options. If the policy prevents you from handling a member's request, suggest other ways to help the member.

Loan policies and procedures will vary among credit unions. When it comes to the rules at your credit union, you *must* know and follow them.

Chapter 7

Conclusion

In this handbook you have found the basic concepts and skills you need to be a successful credit union loan professional. However, your learning does not end here. In fact, it just begins. Each day on the job will bring you new insights into relating with members and coworkers. Experience will be your greatest teacher, as long as you remain open to the lessons it provides. Coworkers, too, will support you, sharing their ideas and knowledge. And management will encourage you, offering advice when necessary.

The purpose of this handbook is to provide you with a foundation for the challenging tasks ahead. Its information and self assessments are designed to equip you with the tools you'll need to start your position confidently.

The rest is up to you. Only you can decide how you will use the information this handbook offers. You're the one who will be working with members every day—listening to their needs, exploring ways to handle their requests and treating them with the courtesy they deserve. It's through you that the credit union's principles of mutual self help and not-for-profit financial service will be fulfilled.

As a credit union loan professional, you hold a unique and valuable position. You have the opportunity to make a substantial contribution to the enrichment of members' lives through the extension of credit. At the same time, you are charged with the responsibility to protect other members' funds. Combining these two roles is a constant challenge

—one that can be met successfully only by mastering the skills and techniques presented in this handbook.

Even after mastering the fundamental skills, your training will not be complete. The lending field is constantly changing. New laws, revised forms and improved credit analysis techniques are just some of the changes you'll see. To update your skills, you'll need additional training. Attending seminars sponsored by your league or Credit Union National Association is one way to keep ahead. You can also sign up for local college classes or use training materials offered by your own credit union.

In any case, the position you've chosen should never become dull. Serving credit union members in the loan department is stimulating, challenging and rewarding. Above all, being a credit union loan professional can be satisfying and enjoyable.

Bibliography

Books

Bruce, Denise. *Cross-selling*. CUNA, Inc., Human Resource Development Department. Dubuque, IA: Kendall/Hunt, 1988. Discusses cross-selling and marketing in credit unions, and the steps to achieving sales success (videocassette and book).

Consumer Finance. CUNA, Inc., Human Resource Development Department. Dubuque, IA: Kendall/Hunt, 1982. Presents concepts of sound financial planning.

Credit Union Business Lending. CUNA, Inc., Human Resource Development Department. Madison, WI: 1987. Provides information on policies, procedures, and loan administration; includes summary of NCUA regulations.

Credit Union Credit Committee Handbook. CUNA, Inc., Human Resource Development Department. Dubuque, IA: Kendall/Hunt, 1990. Provides introduction to credit committee duties and responsibilities; includes self assessments.

Dennis, Marshall W. *Residential Mortgage Lending*, 2nd edition. Englewood Cliffs, NJ: Prentice Hall, 1989. Explains the fundamentals of residential mortgage lending.

Home Equity Lending Guide. CUNA, Inc., Human Resource Development Department. Madison, WI: 1989 (with 1990 addendum). Explains procedures for starting a home equity lending program with explanations of pertinent regulations.

Lee, James and Pulvino, Charles. *Financial Counseling: Interviewing Skills*. CUNA, Inc., Human Resource Development Department. Dubuque, IA: Kendall/Hunt, 1980. Discusses principles and practices of counseling with guidelines for establishing a financial counseling program.

Introduction to Credit Unions, 4th edition. CUNA, Inc., Human Resource Development Department. Dubuque, IA: Kendall/Hunt, 1990. Discusses the history and philosophy of credit unions, structure of the system, leadership duties and responsibilities, and demographics; includes glossary, directories, and references.

Rohner, Ralph J. *The Law of Truth in Lending*. Boston, MA: Warren, Gorham & Lamont, Inc., 1984. Complete legal reference with periodic supplements.

Serian, Robert. *Bankruptcy: A Credit Union Guide to Prevention and Recovery*. CUNA, Inc., Human Resource Development Department. Madison, WI: 1989. Provides explanation of bankruptcy system and abuse, with procedures to avoid bankruptcy filings; worksheets, checklists, forms included.

Magazines and Reprints

"A credit union glossary," *Credit Union Magazine* reprint, Madison, WI: CUNA, 1988. Explains more than 1,000 credit union and financial words, abbreviations and acronyms.

Credit Union Magazine. Madison, WI: Publications Department, CUNA. A monthly magazine for volunteers, officials and employees of credit unions, with features for and about credit unions. (Includes "Lending Letter" column.)

"Credit union history and philosophy," *Credit Union Magazine* reprint, Madison, WI: CUNA, 1989. A series of articles showing how the unique principles of credit unions relate to today's operations.

See also various titles in the *Staff Recognition and Training Program*, available through your league or the Human Resource Development Department, Credit Union National Association, Madison, WI.

Notes

Notes

Notes

Notes

Notes

3 1382 00202 4573

Notes

OC HG 2037 .S38 1991

Sauber, Mary Anne.
Credit union loan
professional handbook
#26056109 2/94

-7210